GUTSY GIRLS
GO FOR
SCIENCE
Programmers

WITH STEM PROJECTS
for KIDS

KAREN BUSH GIBSON
Illustrated by Shululu

EXPLORE QR CONNECTIONS!
You can use a smartphone or tablet app to scan the
QR codes and explore more! Cover up neighboring QR
codes to make sure you're scanning the right one.
You can find a list of urls on the Resources page.

If the QR code doesn't work, try searching the internet with
the Keyword Prompts to find other helpful sources.

Connect . . . . 🔎 programming

Nomad Press
A division of Nomad Communications
10 9 8 7 6 5 4 3 2 1

This book was manufactured by CGB Printers, North Mankato, Minnesota, United States

September 2019, Job #280811

ISBN Softcover: 978-1-61930-789-6
ISBN Hardcover: 978-1-61930-786-5

Educational Consultant, Marla Conn

Questions regarding the ordering of this book should be addressed to
Nomad Press
2456 Christian St., White River Junction, VT 05001
www.nomadpress.net

Printed in the United States.

Books in the **Gutsy Girls Go for Science** series explore career connections for young scientists!

Other books in the series include:

Explore the lives of some of the world's most amazing female astronauts: Bonnie Dunbar, Sally Ride, Mae Jemison, Sunita Williams, and Serena Auñón-Chancellor are all pioneers in the field of space exploration.

PB: 978-1-61930-781-0, $14.95
HC: 978-1-61930-778-0, $19.95
eBook: all formats available, $9.99

Meet five female paleontologists who made breakthrough discoveries of ancient life from millions of years ago, including Mary Anning, Mignon Talbot, Tilly Edinger, Zofia Kielan-Jaworowska, and Mary Leakey.

PB: 978-1-61930-793-3, $14.95
HC: 978-1-61930-790-2, $19.95
eBook: all formats available, $9.99

Meet five female engineers who revolutionized the role of women in engineering, including Ellen Swallow Richards, Emily Warren Roebling, Kate Gleason, Lillian Moller Gilbreth, and Mary Jackson.

PB: 978-1-61930-785-8, $14.95
HC: 978-1-61930-782-7, $19.95
eBook: all formats available, $9.99

CONTENTS

47 THE ENIAC WOMEN

Unsung Heroes

Very few people knew that a group of six women were responsible for programming the ENIAC.

63 DOROTHY VAUGHAN

Early NASA Programmer

This woman conquered other people's opinions on gender and race to become NASA's first African American supervisor.

MARGARET HAMILTON 81

Programming to the Moon

Without Margaret's programming know-how, astronauts might have never made it to the moon!

INTRODUCTION

HELLO WORLD!

1

Computer Talk

A CAR STOPS AS A TRAFFIC LIGHT CHANGES TO RED.

When the light turns green, it means the car can go. Red equals stop. Green equals go. It's a simple set of instructions that the traffic light—and the traffic!—follows.

This an example of code used in everyday life. Code is a way of transferring information between people and machines. A programmer used code to tell the traffic light what to do. It is the language of computerized devices. And it's one of the most powerful types of communication today.

Do you have computers or laptops at your school? What about a smartphone? All of these devices that we use every day rely on programming to work.

Digital devices can go places that people can't go—inside hurricanes, to the ocean floor, and beyond the solar system. The programs that are part of these devices make all this possible.

Without programs, computers wouldn't know what to do. Programmers use a step-by-step approach to solve a problem. Every app a smartphone uses, every job a computer does, every turn a Mars rover makes, a programmer had to write a set of instructions to make it possible. Sound like a lot of work? It is.

NASA's *Curiosity* Mars rover uses its programming to explore a planet where humans can't yet survive for long periods of time.

credit: NASA/JPL-Caltech/MSSS

BC—Before Computers!

It's hard to imagine life without computers, but 100 years ago, that's exactly what life was like—no computers.

People did things manually, even when it took a long time. That includes doing long math problems (no calculators), waiting for film to be exposed in early cameras (no selfies), and using paper maps (no GPS).

COMPUTER CAREERS

Who works with computers? About 62 percent of Americans use the internet in their jobs. About 4 million people work in the computer science and information industry. Programming and software engineering are some of the highest-demand careers today. More than half a million new computer and information jobs are expected to exist in the United States by 2026.

Humans are always looking for new ways to do things faster and better. As time went on, people changed the way they made products. Companies opened factories, where many products could be produced at the same time. And machines helped with the job!

An abacus is an early counting machine!

Once engineers invented circuits, computers began to go digital. People learned to program those digital computers to do different things in different areas. The U.S. military was one of the first users of computers. These early computers, built in the 1940s, took up entire rooms! They took much more time to use than the computers we have today.

COMPUTER RICE

Today, there is a computer the size of a grain of rice. The Michigan Micro Mote can take pictures, read data, and record information. Researchers are still experimenting, but they hope that the tiny computers could be injected into a human body to check temperature and identify possible health problems.

The ENIAC computer in 1946. That's a big computer!

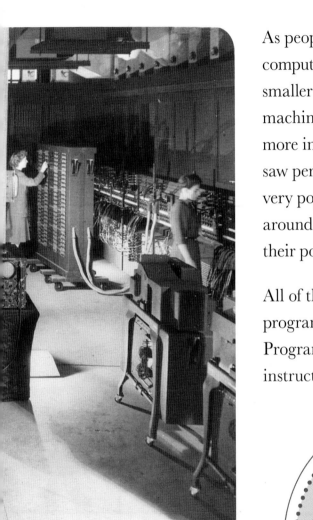

As people worked on the design of computers and found ways to make them smaller and faster and cheaper, these machines began to appear more and more in businesses and homes. The 1980s saw personal computers, or PCs, become very popular. Today, many people walk around with a very small computer in their pockets—a smartphone!

All of these computers and computer programs need programmers. Programmers give computers specific instructions on what to do.

As calculators became more advanced, they became smaller. We've seen the same thing happen with computers. Why? Is smaller better?

W onder **h** y **?**

Crack the Code

Computers read binary code, or machine code. A binary digit, also known as a bit, is a building block of information. The most basic code is binary, using a system of zeros (0) and ones (1). The series of 0s and 1s is hard for humans to read, but this is what computers understand.

So how do we get from human language to the computer language made of 0s and 1s? Programmers write instructions in a language called source code, which looks a bit like random words and punctuation, but is actually filled with meaning! This source code is translated into the machine code that computers understand. Sometimes, computer scientists use a program called a compiler to do this.

Have you ever played Minecraft? This computer game is written with a computer language called Java!

Gutsy Girls Go for Science: Programmers

JAVA

PYTHON

HTML

C#

In this book, we'll meet several women who cracked the code of working in the computer field and made technological advances that changed the way we live! You'll learn about Ada Lovelace, Grace Hopper, the six ENIAC women who programmed the first electronic computer, Dorothy Vaughan, and Margaret Hamilton. Ready to get busy? Let's go!

There are lots of vocabulary words in this book!

Try to figure out the meaning by looking at the surrounding sentences or find the definition in the glossary.

Behind the Scenes

WHEN YOU LOOK AT A PAGE ON THE INTERNET, THE CODE ISN'T IMMEDIATELY EVIDENT. BUT THERE ARE WAYS TO SEE THE SOURCE CODE. TAKE A LOOK! ALWAYS GET AN ADULT'S PERMISSION TO USE THE INTERNET.

1 Go to the internet with your favorite browser.

2 Navigate to one of your favorite websites.

3 Examine the elements of the page and how they interact with each other.

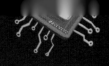

...ee what the code for the web page
...ks like, follow the directions below
...the browser you're using.

CHROME: Right click with your mouse
over a fixed headline. Left click on
"Inspect Element" to see the code.

SAFARI: Enable the Developer menu. Go to
Preferences > Advanced in the Safari menu. Click
"Show Develop menu in menu bar." Close the
Preferences window and go the Develop menu,
where you will click on "Show Page Source."

INTERNET EXPLORER: Press the
Alt key for the browser's menu bar.
Select "View," and "Source" from the
drop-down menu that appears.

EDGE: Click on
the More icon on
the upper-right
hand corner of
your screen. Select
"Developer Tools"
from the drop-down
menu that appears.
You can also reach
it with one of two
shortcuts: pressing
Ctrl+U or F12 on
your keyboard.

Try This!

See how the
web page
code looks different with
different browsers and on
different digital devices.
You'll see similarities,
but also differences,
too! Programmers often
have to see how their
code looks with different
browsers and devices.

Ada Lovelace ·····

> "A new, a vast and a powerful language is developed for the future use of analysis, in which to wield its truths so that these may become of more speedy and accurate practical application for the purposes of mankind."

—Ada Lovelace

Date of Birth:
December 10, 1815

Place of Birth:
London, England

Date of Death:
November 27, 1852, age 36

Famous for:
British mathematician and the world's first computer programmer

The Countess of Computers

HOW DO WE MAKE COMPUTERS DO WHAT WE WANT THEM TO DO?

Programming! Without a shared programming language, humans and computers wouldn't be able to communicate, and computers wouldn't be very useful.

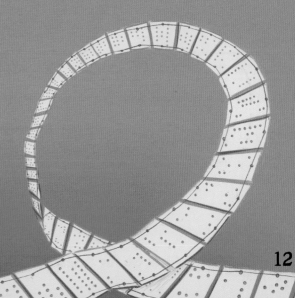

The person considered to be one of the first computer programmers didn't actually work on a computer. She had to use her imagination and write notes on how people could communicate with computers, which hadn't quite been invented yet. But the work she did laid the foundation for future languages that people still use today.

In fact, in the 1970s, the U.S. Department of Defense developed a new programming language named ADA. This language is named after Ada Lovelace, the first computer programmer!

Ada Lovelace

credit: Alfred Edward Chalon

TIMELINE	1815	1828
	Ada Lovelace is born.	Ada designs a flying machine.

As a Kid

A man named Lord Byron was a famous poet in the early 1800s. At a party one day, he met a serious 19-year-old woman named Anabella. Anabella came from a wealthy family. She was passionate about mathematics. Lord Byron gave Anabella the nickname, "Princess of Parallelograms."

Lord Byron and Anabella were married in January of 1815. Nearly a year later, they had a daughter—Augusta Ada Byron. When Ada was five weeks old, she and her mother moved in with her mother's family.

Ada Byron at age four, from a miniature in a locket sent to Lord Byron by his sister, 1819 or 1820

1837	**1843**	**1852**	**1946**	**2009**
The first mechanical, general purpose computer is proposed by Charles Babbage.	Ada publishes a translation with her own notes on the analytical engine. Her published work includes the first computer program.	Ada Lovelace passes away.	The ENIAC becomes the first electronic computer.	The first Ada Lovelace Day is held to celebrate women in STEM throughout the world.

Lord Byron passed away soon after this. His servant later said that Lord Byron's last words were about his daughter.

Ada's mother believed strongly in education for females, and hired tutors to teach her daughter math and science. She didn't want her daughter to follow in Lord Byron's footsteps and become a poet!

Ada had a lonely childhood. She was kept company only by servants, tutors, and a cat named Puff. She was often sick and spent most of her time indoors, reading and studying.

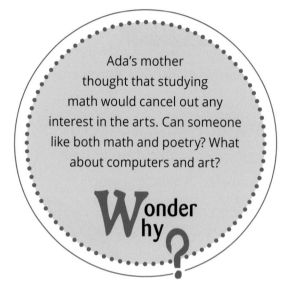

Ada's mother thought that studying math would cancel out any interest in the arts. Can someone like both math and poetry? What about computers and art?

Wonder **hy**?

> **"** Ada! sole daughter of my house and heart? When last I saw thy young blue eyes, they smiled, And then we parted,—not as now we part, But with a hope. **"**
>
> **—Lord Byron**, about his daughter

Ada didn't really mind being alone. She discovered that she could be creative with math and science.

At age 12, she decided she wanted to fly. So, she designed a flying machine. Her machine was shaped like a horse with a steam engine inside to power it. The flying machine came with a pair of mechanical wings based upon those of birds.

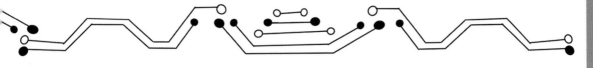

When Ada was 13, she caught the measles and spent three years sick in bed! Her mother encouraged Ada to spend even more time working on her studies, including chemistry.

When Ada got better, she was a little bit rebellious toward her mother. She wanted to learn more than just math and science.

THE WORLD'S FIRST FEMALE MATHEMATICIAN

The first known female mathematician and scientist was Hypatia (c. 370-415). She was born in Alexandria, a great city in Egypt. Her father, Theon, was a mathematician at Alexandria's university. He taught his daughter everything he knew and they often worked together. When Hypatia became an adult, she also taught at the university. She was the only woman known to do so. Hypatia was accomplished at mathematics, astronomy, and philosophy. She was also an inventor and either invented an early astrolabe or improved upon it, researchers aren't sure which.

During Hypatia's time, some people believed that mathematics and witchcraft were the same thing, and dangerous. One day, when Hypatia was leaving the university, she was killed by a mob that felt angry and scared enough to attack a woman who dared to study and learn.

As she grew older and met more people and learned more about the world, Ada noticed a relationship between music and math.

Ada also saw poetry in math and science. She called herself an analyst and metaphysician who studied poetical science. She was fascinated by how the brain creates thoughts.

Ada at age 17

Ada was interested in machines, in particular the Jacquard loom. This weaving machine used punch cards to weave designs in cloth, a detail she wouldn't forget when designing a system of her own.

Gutsy Girls Go for Science: Programmers

66 I think it's very important to get more women into computing. My slogan is: Computing is too important to be left to men. 99

—**Karen Spärck Jones**,
Professor of Computers and
Information at Cambridge
Computer Laboratory

Code.org is an organization that encourages everyone to learn code. Try this one-hour coding activity to create your own Google logo.

Connect . . . . . .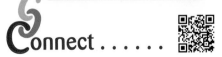

A Meeting of Minds

When Ada was 17, she met Charles Babbage (1791–1871), a mathematics professor at Cambridge University. Charles showed Ada his plans for a small-scale model, called a prototype, of a calculating machine he was working on. He called it a Difference Engine. He envisioned it as a hand-cranked calculator with about 4,000 parts. It would weigh at least 2 tons.

BECOMING COUNTESS

When she was 19, Ada met and married William King. Soon after their marriage, he became an earl, which meant that she became the Countess of Lovelace. Her official name is August Ada Byron King-Noel, Countess of Lovelace. Today, she is most often referred to as Ada Lovelace.

A model of Charles Babbage's Difference Engine in an exhibit at the Computer History Museum

credit: Jitze Couperus (CC BY 2.0)

Ada was excited about the calculating machine. Charles realized that she understood mathematics in a way that few people did. He called her the "Enchantress of Numbers."

The two became friends and wrote frequent letters to each other about mathematics and logic.

Did Ada's wealth give her opportunities that other girls didn't have? If she had been poor, would she still have been so involved in math?

Wonder **Why?**

Visions of a Computer

Now a married countess and mother, Ada kept up with her studies. She even hired a mathematician to teach her trigonometry, the study of triangles.

Meanwhile, Charles began work on his new invention, called an Analytical Engine. While the Difference Engine, which he never actually built, would have produced and calculated rows and columns of numbers, the Analytical Engine was to be able to solve math problems and store information.

Ada Lovelace, 1836

credit: Margaret Sarah Carpenter

Ada Lovelace Day is held the second Tuesday in October each year. It's a day of recognition for women in science, technology, engineering, and math—known as STEM.

Ada could see that such a machine could work with anything—words, graphics, and music. Just like the computers we have today!

Charles Babbage delivered talks about his ideas for the Analytical Engine to many different groups. After one of those talks, an Italian engineer and mathematician wrote a paper in French about Babbage's machine. It's not clear whether translating the paper into English was Charles's idea or Ada's, but she was excited to take on the job!

Charles Babbage, 1871

credit: Unknown staff artist for *The Illustrated London News*

Ada's translation included her own notes describing the machine and how it would work. A series of instructions, or algorithms, could be programmed into the machine with punch cards.

> *Ada explained that the Analytical Engine could weave patterns "just as the Jacquard loom weaves flowers and leaves."*

Her "Notes" section was more than twice as long as the original 8,000-word paper. Perhaps more importantly, she figured out an algorithm that the machine could use.

Some of Ada's notes on the Analytical Engine

Diagram for

Number of Operation.	Nature of Operation.	Variables acted upon.	Variables receiving results.	Indication of change in the value on any Variable.	Statement of Results.
1	$\times$	$^1V_2 \times ^1V_3$	$^1V_4, ^1V_5, ^1V_6$	$\begin{cases} ^1V_2 = ^1V_2 \\ ^1V_3 = ^1V_3 \end{cases}$	$= 2n$
2	$-$	$^1V_4 - ^1V_1$	$^2V_4$	$\begin{cases} ^1V_4 = ^2V_4 \\ ^1V_1 = ^1V_1 \end{cases}$	$= 2n - 1$
3	$+$	$^1V_5 + ^1V_1$	$^2V_5$	$\begin{cases} ^1V_5 = ^2V_5 \\ ^1V_1 = ^1V_1 \end{cases}$	$= 2n + 1$
4	$\div$	$^2V_5 \div ^2V_4$	$^1V_{11}$	$\begin{cases} ^2V_5 = ^0V_5 \\ ^2V_4 = ^0V_4 \end{cases}$	$= \dfrac{2n-1}{2n+1}$
5	$\div$	$^1V_{11} \div ^1V_2$	$^2V_{11}$	$\begin{cases} ^1V_{11} = ^2V_{11} \\ ^1V_2 = ^1V_2 \end{cases}$	$= \dfrac{1}{2} \cdot \dfrac{2n-1}{2n+1}$
6	$-$	$^0V_{13} - ^2V_{11}$	$^1V_{13}$	$\begin{cases} ^2V_{11} = ^0V_{11} \\ ^0V_{13} = ^1V_{13} \end{cases}$	$= -\dfrac{1}{2} \cdot \dfrac{2n-1}{2n+1} = A_0$
7	$-$	$^1V_3 - ^1V_1$	$^1V_{10}$	$\begin{cases} ^1V_3 = ^1V_3 \\ ^1V_1 = ^1V_1 \end{cases}$	$= n - 1 (= 3)$
8	$+$	$^1V_2 + ^0V_7$	$^1V_7$	$\begin{cases} ^1V_2 = ^1V_2 \\ ^0V_7 = ^1V_7 \end{cases}$	$= 2 + 0 = 2$
9	$\div$	$^1V_6 + ^1V_7$	$^3V_{11}$	$\begin{cases} ^1V_6 = ^1V_6 \\ ^0V_{11} = ^3V_{11} \end{cases}$	$= \dfrac{2n}{2} = A_1$
10	$\times$	$^1V_{21} \times ^3V_{11}$	$^1V_{12}$	$\begin{cases} ^1V_{21} = ^1V_{21} \\ ^3V_{11} = ^3V_{11} \end{cases}$	$= B_1 \cdot \dfrac{2n}{2} = B_1 A_1$
11	$+$	$^1V_{12} + ^1V_{13}$	$^2V_{13}$	$\begin{cases} ^1V_{12} = ^0V_{12} \\ ^1V_{13} = ^2V_{13} \end{cases}$	$= -\dfrac{1}{2} \cdot \dfrac{2n-1}{2n+1} + B_1 \cdot \dfrac{2}{2}$
12	$-$	$^1V_{10} - ^1V_1$	$^2V_{10}$	$\begin{cases} ^1V_{10} = ^2V_{10} \\ ^1V_1 = ^1V_1 \end{cases}$	$= n - 2 (= 2)$
13	$-$	$^1V_6 - ^1V_1$	$^2V_6$	$\begin{cases} ^1V_6 = ^2V_6 \\ ^1V_1 = ^1V_1 \end{cases}$	$= 2n - 1$
14	$+$	$^1V_1 + ^1V_7$	$^2V_7$	$\begin{cases} ^1V_1 = ^1V_1 \\ ^1V_7 = ^2V_7 \end{cases}$	$= 2 + 1 = 3$
15	$\div$	$^2V_6 + ^2V_7$	$^1V_8$	$\begin{cases} ^2V_6 = ^2V_6 \\ ^2V_7 = ^2V_7 \end{cases}$	$= \dfrac{2n-1}{3}$
16	$\times$	$^1V_8 \times ^3V_{11}$	$^4V_{11}$	$\begin{cases} ^1V_8 = ^0V_8 \\ ^3V_{11} = ^4V_{11} \end{cases}$	$= \dfrac{2n}{2} \cdot \dfrac{2n-1}{3}$
17	$-$	$^2V_6 - ^1V_1$	$^3V_6$	$\begin{cases} ^2V_6 = ^3V_6 \\ ^1V_1 = ^1V_1 \end{cases}$	$= 2n - 2$
18	$+$	$^1V_1 + ^2V_7$	$^3V_7$	$\begin{cases} ^2V_7 = ^3V_7 \\ ^1V_1 = ^1V_1 \end{cases}$	$= 3 + 1 = 4$
19	$\div$	$^3V_6 + ^3V_7$	$^1V_9$	$\begin{cases} ^3V_6 = ^3V_6 \\ ^3V_7 = ^3V_7 \end{cases}$	$= \dfrac{2n-2}{4}$
20	$\times$	$^1V_9 \times ^4V_{11}$	$^5V_{11}$	$\begin{cases} ^1V_9 = ^0V_9 \\ ^4V_{11} = ^5V_{11} \end{cases}$	$= \dfrac{2n}{2} \cdot \dfrac{2n-1}{3} \cdot \dfrac{2n-2}{4}$
21	$\times$	$^1V_{22} \times ^5V_{11}$	$^0V_{12}$	$\begin{cases} ^1V_{22} = ^1V_{22} \\ ^0V_{12} = ^2V_{12} \end{cases}$	$= B_3 \cdot \dfrac{2n}{2} \cdot \dfrac{2n-1}{3} \cdot \dfrac{2n-2}{3}$
22	$+$	$^2V_{12} + ^2V_{13}$	$^3V_{13}$	$\begin{cases} ^2V_{12} = ^0V_{12} \\ ^2V_{13} = ^3V_{13} \end{cases}$	$= A_0 + B_1 A_1 + B_3 A_3$
23	$-$	$^2V_{10} - ^1V_1$	$^3V_{10}$	$\begin{cases} ^2V_{10} = ^3V_{10} \\ ^1V_1 = ^1V_1 \end{cases}$	$= n - 3 (= 1)$
24	$+$	$^4V_{13} + ^0V_{24}$	$^1V_{24}$	$\begin{cases} ^4V_{13} = ^0V_{13} \\ ^0V_{24} = ^1V_{24} \end{cases}$	$= B_7$
25	$+$	$^1V_1 + ^1V_3$	$^1V_3$	$\begin{cases} ^1V_1 = ^1V_1 \\ ^1V_3 = ^1V_3 \\ ^5V_6 = ^0V_6 \\ ^5V_7 = ^0V_7 \end{cases}$	$= n + 1 = 4 + 1 = 5$ by a Variable-card. by a Variable card.

Gutsy Girls Go for Science: Programmers

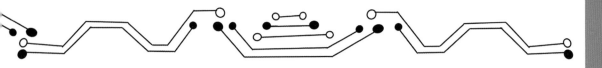

by the Engine of the Numbers of Bernoulli. See Note G. (page 722 *et seq.*)

									Working Variables.								Result Variables.			
${}^4V_3$	${}^0V_4$	${}^0V_5$	${}^0V_6$	${}^0V_7$	${}^0V_8$	${}^0V_9$	${}^0V_{10}$	${}^0V_{11}$	${}^0V_{12}$	${}^0V_{13}$	${}^1V_{21}$	${}^1V_{22}$	${}^1V_{23}$	${}^0V_{24}$...
○	○	○	○	○	○	○	○	○	○	○	○	○	○	○
0	0	0	0	0	0	0	0	0	0	0	B_1 in a decimal fraction. 0	B_3 in a decimal fraction. 0	B_5 in a decimal fraction. 0	0
0	0	0	0	0	0	0	0	0	0	0	0	0	0	0
4	0	0	0	0	0	0	0	0	0	0	0	0	0	0
n	□	□	□	□	□	□	□	□	□	□	B_1	B_3	B_5	B_7
n	$2n$	$2n$	$2n$											
...	$2n-1$													
...	...	$2n+1$												
...	0	0	...					$\dfrac{2n-1}{2n+1}$						
...	...	...	...					$\dfrac{1}{2}\cdot\dfrac{2n-1}{2n+1}$						
...	...	...	...					0						
n	...	...	...				$n-1$		....	$-\dfrac{1}{2}\cdot\dfrac{2n-1}{2n+1}=A_0$				
...	...	...	...	2										
...	...	$2n$	$2n$	2				$\dfrac{2n}{2}=A_1$						
...	...	...	...	...				$\dfrac{2n}{2}=A_1$	$B_1\cdot\dfrac{2n}{2}=B_1A_1$	....	B_1			
...	...	...	...	...				....	0	$\left\{-\dfrac{1}{2}\dfrac{2n-1}{2n+1}+B_1\cdot\dfrac{2n}{2}\right\}$				
...	...	...	...	...			$n-2$							
...	...	$2n-1$												
...	...	...		3										
...	...	$2n-1$		3	$\dfrac{2n-1}{3}$									
...	...	...	...	...	0	...	...	$\dfrac{2n}{2}\cdot\dfrac{2n-1}{3}$						
...	...	$2n-2$												
...	...	...		4										
...	...	$2n-2$		4		$\dfrac{2n-2}{4}$	...	$\left\{\dfrac{2n}{2}\cdot\dfrac{2n-1}{3}\cdot\dfrac{2n-2}{3}=A_3\right\}$						
...	...	...	...	...		0								
...	...	...	...	...				0	B_3A_2	....		B_3		
...	...	...	...	...					0	$\left\{A_3+B_1A_1+B_3A_3\right\}$				
...	...	...	...	...			$n-3$							

Here follows a repetition of Operations thirteen to twenty-three.

$n+1$	...	...	0	0				...	....	....	......	......	......	B_7

Remember, an algorithm is a process or set of rules to follow in calculations and in solving problems. What does this sound like? If you guessed programming, you're right! This is why Ada Lovelace is recognized as the world's first programmer.

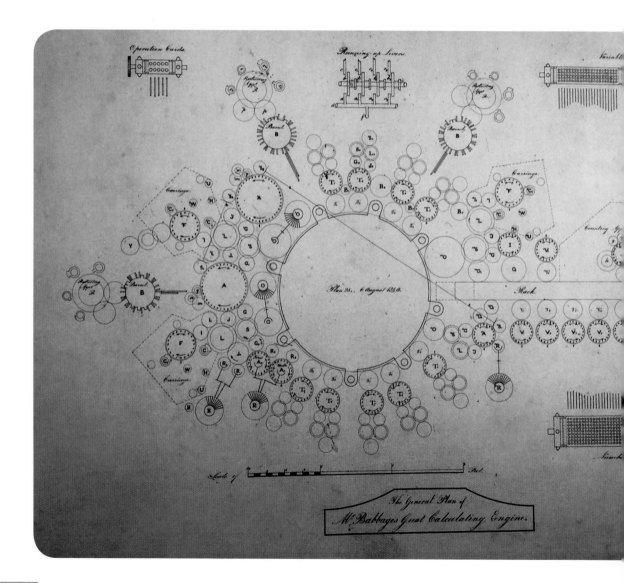

When computers were first built during the twentieth century, inventors studied Charles's designs and Ada's notes.

Charles Babbage's plan for the Analytical Engine

credit: photo taken by ArnoldReinhold (CC BY 4.0)

The article, *Sketch of the Analytical Engine Invented by Charles Babbage* was published in 1843 when Ada was just 27 years old. She began experiencing health problems soon afterward. She passed away from cancer at age 36 on November 27, 1852. At her request, she was buried next to her father.

Sydney Padua is a cartoonist and graphic artist. In addition to her work on graphic novels, she publishes a webcomic about Ada Lovelace and has turned it into a graphic novel. To read some samples of *Sydney Padua's Thrilling Adventures of Lovelace and Babbage*, check out this website.

Connect . . . .

🔎 Sydney Padua Lovelace

Breaking It Down

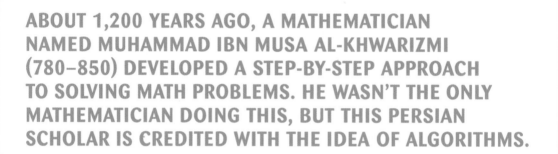

ABOUT 1,200 YEARS AGO, A MATHEMATICIAN NAMED MUHAMMAD IBN MUSA AL-KHWARIZMI (780–850) DEVELOPED A STEP-BY-STEP APPROACH TO SOLVING MATH PROBLEMS. HE WASN'T THE ONLY MATHEMATICIAN DOING THIS, BUT THIS PERSIAN SCHOLAR IS CREDITED WITH THE IDEA OF ALGORITHMS.

An algorithm is a set of steps to follow in order to accomplish a task. It has a beginning and an end. Algorithms can be followed by humans or machines.

Programmers break complicated tasks into smaller, step-by-step tasks. These step-by-step instructions are algorithms. Each piece of code directs the computer to perform one step or instruction. Algorithms transform information and automate tasks. They make code more efficient.

When you do a division problem in math class, you solve the problem with an algorithm. Here's an example.

A simple question such as 84 divided by 6 might have the following algorithm.

- How many times does 6 go into 8? (The answer is 1)

- How many is left over? (2)

- Bring the numbers at the top, down (In this example, drop the 4 next to the 2)

- How many times does 6 go into 24? (The answer is 4)

84 divided by 6 is 14. The answer is reached by following an algorithm.

Now it's your turn to write an algorithm.

1 Choose a task you do every day.

2 Write down a step-by-step set of instructions that will be clear enough for someone to follow. Remember to consider different decisions someone has to make and how these decisions will affect the final outcome.

3 Ask a friend or family member to follow your algorithm. Are they successful?

Try This!

Revise! Computer programmers spend many hours revising their codes to get them just right. What do you need to change or add to your algorithm to make it easier to follow?

GRACE MURRAY HOPPER

> " The only phrase I've ever disliked is, 'Why, we've always done it that way.' I always tell young people, go ahead and do it. You can always apologize later. "
>
> —Grace Hopper

Date of Birth:	Place of Birth:	Date of Death:	Famous for:
December 9, 1906	New York, New York	January 1, 1992, age 85	Developed first compiler, also developed the first programming language used for business

Queen of Code

NO DOUBT YOU'VE HEARD OF COMPUTER BUGS.

Most people have. A computer bug is an error in a computer program that causes it to produce an incorrect or unexpected result. Why do we call these bugs?

30

Commodore Grace M. Hopper, 1984

0800   antan started
1000   stopped - antan ✓
    13'ec (032) MP - MC
    (033) PRO 2   2.
    conect   2.1
    Relays 6-2 in 033
    In Relay

1700 Started Cosine Tape
1525 Started Mult + Adder

1545   Rel
    (mot

First actual case of
1630 antangent started.
1700 closed down.

TIMELINE

1906
Grace Murray is born on December 9.

1944
The Mark I computer is completed in the United States.

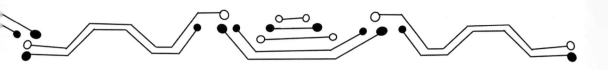

In 1947, a moth was found in the Mark II computer. The bug had short circuited a relay, which is an electronic switch. Grace Murray Hopper taped it to the computer logbook and wrote, "first actual case of bug being found." She was the first to talk of "debugging" computers! She was also the first to do many things.

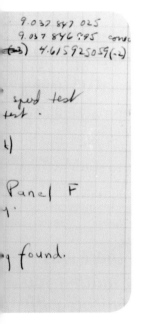

As a Kid

Grace Brewster Murray was born in New York City on December 9, 1906. Even as a child, she always wanted to know how things worked.

Clocks, for example. Where did the ticking come from? When Grace was seven, she decided to find out, so she took apart one clock, then another, and another.

1946	1952	1957	1959	1992
ENIAC becomes the first electronic digital computer.	Grace develops the first compiler.	FORTRAN programming language is developed by a team at IBM.	A team led by Grace develops COBOL, a business-oriented programming language.	Grace passes away on January 1.

She was one of four women entering Yale's Ph.D. program in mathematics. While there, she married Vincent Foster Hopper and changed her last name.

After earning a PhD in 1934, Grace Hopper began teaching mathematics at Vassar. She approached teaching the same way she approached life—with a desire to shake things up. She wanted her students to study writing and science as well as math.

Grace believed there was no use learning math if you couldn't communicate with others, and she saw writing as a link among the different subjects.

This didn't make Grace very popular with other professors, but the students loved her.

In 1930, 15 percent of math doctorates in the United States were women. By the 1950s, that number had dropped to 4 percent. It took more than 50 years for that percentage to rise to the level it had been in 1930. Why do you think this is?

Wonder **hy?**

The Murrays were a prosperous family who lived in Manhattan and spent their summers at a lake in New Hampshire. Books were plentiful at the Murray house. The family valued education.

Grace started at Vassar College at age 17. By 1928, she had math and physics degrees. She continued her education at Yale, earning an advanced degree in mathematics by the time she was 23.

GIRLS ONLY!

Vassar began in 1861 as a college for women. Back then, most colleges and universities didn't allow women to attend, so sometimes, people began new schools for girls. Vassar had the reputation for being very challenging. Women could take classes in art history, geology, astronomy, music, mathematics, and chemistry. It was known as a school that offered experiential learning. In 1869, the famous astronomer Maria Mitchell took her students out of the state to observe an eclipse of the sun! Vassar allowed boys to enroll in 1969. What do you think might have changed when men began to attend?

The entrance to Vassar College, 1904

Wartime

The Japanese attacked Pearl Harbor, Hawaii, on December 7, 1941, and the next day, the United States entered World War II. American women and men wanted to serve their country. But there weren't many opportunities for women.

Grace wanted to do her part as well. Her great-grandfather had been a rear admiral in the Navy, so she tried to join the Navy. But at 35 years old and 108 pounds, she was considered too old and too small.

Grace's determination, which would become famous through her career, pushed her. She kept applying until she was finally accepted into the WAVES, or Women Accepted for Volunteer Emergency Service.

When Grace enlisted, there were approximately 27,000 WAVES. There would be more than three times that number by the end of the war.

HEDY LAMARR (1914–2000)

Grace Hopper isn't the only woman to revolutionize technology for the Navy. If you're a fan of old movies, the name Hedy Lamarr might be familiar. She was a famous movie actress in the 1940s and 1950s. She also developed technology that makes today's wireless technology possible. Torpedoes in wartime were successful only 40 percent of the time because the radio signals jammed up. Single-frequency settings also left ships vulnerable to attack. Hedy worked with a composer friend on a way for a sender and receiver to hop frequencies in a pattern. She patented the invention, and then gave it to the Navy. The Navy didn't use Hedy's invention during World War II, but they did use the technology in the late 1950s. In 1990, Hedy's invention became public and was used for all kinds of things we have today, including satellite technology.

Grace Meets Mark I

In 1944, Grace was sent to work at the top-secret Harvard Computational Lab. She was not entirely sure what to expect. An armed guard escorted her to the basement.

The first thing she probably noticed when she walked into the room was the enormous computer. It was 8 feet high and 3 feet wide. At 51 feet long, it weighed about 5 tons. Grace immediately wanted to take it apart and figure out how it worked, just the way she did with those clocks when she was a kid!

"Where have you been?" someone asked as she stared at the computer. That was Howard Aiken (1900–1973). He had expected Grace months earlier, and he hadn't been happy to be assigned a female assistant in the first place. That would soon change.

" If Wright is flight, and Edison is light, then Hopper is code. "

—President Obama, awarding the Presidential Medal of Freedom to Grace

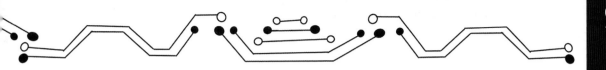

Howard had built that giant computer, called the Automatic Sequence Controlled Calculator. Better known as the Mark I, it was the first in a series of early computers for the military. The Navy would use it to program rocket trajectories and solve engineering problems.

Grace got to work immediately. She was given a notebook of instructional codes for the Mark I. She studied blueprints at night. She learned how to communicate with the machine to get it to do what she wanted.

Grace was the third person to program the Mark I and soon became chief programmer. She also worked on later versions of the computer, the Mark II and Mark III. She wrote the first programming manual—500 pages on the history of the Mark I and how to program it.

When the war ended in 1945, Grace had caught her own computer bug! She decided to stay at Harvard's Computational Laboratory.

Programming Leader

After a few years, it became clear to Grace that Harvard wasn't going to give her tenure and the Navy wasn't going to give her a regular commission. This meant she couldn't count on always having a job. So, she left Harvard in 1949 to go to work for a private company.

Grace was involved in developing early programming languages. She knew that programming was key to making computers more user-friendly to non-mathematicians. If computers were easier to use, more people would use them. She shared code and programming information with other programmers.

Grace realized that computers needed a translator in order to take human commands and turn them into computer language. This is now called a compiler.

When Grace developed the first computer language compiler, she sent it to other programmers for their input.

Another compiler Grace worked on led to the development of a programming language still in use today. Called COBOL, it was the first widely used computer program containing words. It became one of the most frequently used programming languages in the world.

Grace Hopper believe collaboration would make programming better, so she regularly shared her work with others. Do you agree with this approach? What place does competition have in the business of developing computers?

Wonder **hy** ?

A Short Retirement

In the 1960s, Grace retired from the Naval Reserve. It would be a very short retirement. In 1967, the Navy asked her back to lead a project that would standardize programming languages so everyone could use them.

Grace had a clock in her office that ran counterclockwise instead of clockwise. It reminded her not to do things only because that was the way they had always been done.

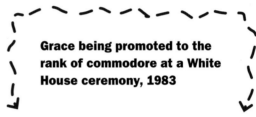

Grace being promoted to the rank of commodore at a White House ceremony, 1983

Five years later, she was 66 and past the age when many people retired. She was also past the age when many people were promoted. But a special vote of the U.S. Congress promoted her to captain. She was later promoted to commodore and then rear admiral.

When Grace retired from the Navy in 1986, she was just a few months from her 80th birthday. She was the oldest-serving officer in all of the armed forces. The highest honor from the U.S. Department of Defense, the Defense Distinguished Service Medal, was presented to her. Grace passed away in 1992.

Grace had many nicknames. Among them, "Amazing Grace," "Grand Lady of Software," and the "Queen of Code."

> **"** If you ask me what accomplishment I'm most proud of, the answer would be all the young people I've trained over the years; that's more important than writing the first compiler. **"**

—Admiral Grace Hopper,
after receiving the National
Medal of Technology

Listen to Grace teach about nanoseconds on this video! Can you see why she was such a popular teacher?

Connect . . . .

🔍 Grace Hopper nanosecond

It's Time to Scratch

DO YOU SPEAK MORE THAN ONE LANGUAGE? SPANISH, FRENCH, FARSI, CHINESE? COMPUTER PROGRAMMING LANGUAGES ARE SIMILAR TO HUMAN LANGUAGES. THEY OFTEN MEAN THE SAME THINGS, BUT SAY IT IN DIFFERENT WAYS. THE DIFFERENCE IS THAT SPECIFIC PROGRAMMING LANGUAGES ARE USUALLY GOOD AT DIFFERENT THINGS.

Scratch is a beginning coding program that can be used to create graphic stories and games. It is used in more than 150 countries, both in schools and in homes. Although it was designed for kids 8 to 16, anyone can use it. Even your parents or grandparents! It is a free program from the MIT Media Lab.

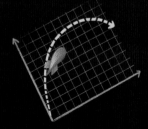

YOUR FIELD KIT CHECKLIST

✓ **COMPUTER WITH INTERNET CONNECTION**

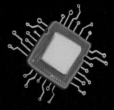

INSTRUCTIONS

1 Go to scratch.mit.edu. Look around the Scratch website.

2 Click on "Explore" at the top of the page to see some examples of what can be done in Scratch.

Another good section is the Tips section. It contains tutorials, activity cards, and guides.

3 If you like what you see, click "Join" on the top right of the page. This will allow you to save your work on the Scratch site. Since it is web-based, you can sign in from any computer to work on your project or show it to someone else.

Try This!

Now it's time for you to create! Click "Create" at the upper left of the page. You'll see a block of tips on your right with tabs. There are step-by-step instructions, how-tos, and information about blocks. What are you going to create? Share it with your family and friends when your done! Maybe they will want to join you in learning code.

Jean Jennings Bartik
(1924–2011)
Born:
Alanthus Grove, Missouri

Betty Snyder Holberton
(1917–2001)
Born:
Philadelphia,
Pennsylvania

Kay McNulty Mauchly Antonelli
(1921–2006)
Born:
County Donegal, Ireland

THE ENIAC WOMEN

" We were sure this machine could do anything we wanted it to do. We were very cocky about that. "

—**Marlyn Wescoff Meltzer**,
one of the ENIAC programmers

45

Marlyn Wescoff Meltzer
(1922–2008)
Born:
Philadelphia,
Pennsylvania

Frances Bilas Spencer
(1922–2012)
Born:
Philadelphia,
Pennsylvania

Ruth Lichterman
Teitelbaum
(1924–1986)
Born:
New York,
New York

Famous for:
The original
programmers for
ENIAC, the first
electronic digital
computer

Unsung Heroes

ON VALENTINE'S DAY IN 1946, MANY REPORTERS WEREN'T THINKING ABOUT THE HOLIDAY.

They were thinking about a demonstration of the first electronic digital computer. A U.S. Army project, it was described as a mathematical robot working at superfast speeds. It was called the Electronic Numerical Integrator and Computer, or ENIAC. It was a revolutionary step.

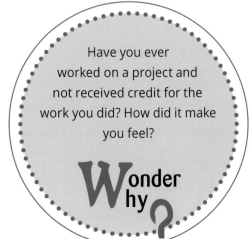

The next day, *The New York Times* featured the ENIAC on the front page of the newspaper. Articles and quotes from the men involved with the project were included in the article.

Have you ever worked on a project and not received credit for the work you did? How did it make you feel?

Wonder Why?

Ruth and Marlyn program ENIAC

TIMELINE

1943
Development of the ENIAC begins.

1944
Colossus machines used in Great Britain solve Nazi codes during World War II. Codes that once took weeks to break now typically take hours.

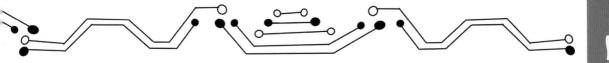

Based on the headlines, you might never know that six women were part of the success of ENIAC. But if you look at the pictures, you'll see them working on ENIAC in the background. Who were these unnamed women? What were they doing?

As Kids

Jean Jennings was born on a Missouri farm outside of Alanthus Grove, population 104. She was the sixth of seven children! She grew up doing lots of farm chores.

Jean lived in a rural area where most people didn't have much money. But the Jennings family knew what was important—education. Jean's father taught in a one-room schoolhouse. Jean's mother tutored students in algebra and geometry.

All the Jennings children went to college. Jean went to Northwest Missouri State Teachers College in Mayville. Tuition was $76 a year. She thought she might like to be a journalist, but didn't care for her adviser, so she switched to math.

1945	1946	1997	2008	2013
World War II ends.	ENIAC is announced to the public. The role of women is overlooked.	The ENIAC women are inducted into the Women in Technology Hall of Fame.	The Computer History Museum honors Jean Bartik with its Fellows Award.	*The Computers*, a documentary about the ENIAC women, is released.

Female Mathematicians Wanted

Many women who attended college during this time period majored in math. And most became teachers. That would probably have been Jean's path as well, except that her calculus teacher showed her a flyer.

Wanted: Women with Degrees in Mathematics

The University of Pennsylvania was looking for female mathematicians. The women would work as "computers," doing a lot of the math that was required at the department.

Jean applied and was accepted. She left on a midnight train, arriving 40 hours later in Pennsylvania. She was 20 years old. It was the first time she had ever been out of Missouri!

At work, Jean sat in a large room with almost 100 other women.

Gutsy Girls Go for Science: Programmers

Pads of paper and desktop adding machines
with cranks lay on the desks. Their job?
Calculating trajectory tables for the
Army.

Back then, missile accuracy was
poor. It depended on many
things, including humidity,
the curve of the earth,
and geography. All of
these things could be
accounted for with math,
but the equations were
complex. It might take
12 hours for one person
to complete one equation!
And it took about a month
for a single ballistics table
to be completed, even
though the women worked as
efficiently as they could.

CODING IN WARTIME: JOAN CLARKE

Joan Clarke (1917–1996) was a codebreaker who played a critical role in cracking the codes of Nazi Germany. This saved countless lives in Great Britain during World War II. Joan was recruited in 1939 by the British government because of her work in mathematics at Cambridge. She and others worked on the Colossus at Bletchley Park, which is now a museum. Take a look!

Women with the Colossus

onnect . . . .

🔎 Bletchley Park

A few months after Jean started her job, a memo came out stating that there were six openings to work on a new machine at the University of Pennsylvania's Moore School of Engineering.

Jean was getting a little bored with her job, so she applied. During her interview, she was asked what she knew about electricity. What they really wanted to know was whether she was scared of electricity. She said she wasn't and was hired.

Gutsy Girls Go for Science: Programmers

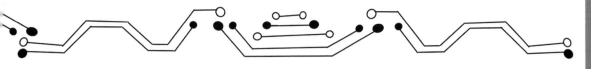

So were five other women: Marlyn Wescoff, Ruth Lichterman, Betty Snyder, Frances Bilas, and Kay McNulty. They came from different backgrounds and cultures. What did they have in common? Math.

Introducing ENIAC

Physicist John Mauchly (1907–1980) had thought up an all-electronic calculating machine in 1942. He correctly believed that it would run faster without mechanical parts. And in wartime, speed was critical. ENIAC was the result, built between 1943 to 1945.

Once the machine was built, it needed to be programmed. The men who'd built it believed that the programming wasn't as important. The six women who'd been hired were called the "ENIAC girls." They received $2,000 a year, plus a $400 bonus for working Saturdays.

The women were sent to an Army facility to learn how to use IBM punch cards and wire up control panels. They returned to the University of Pennsylvania six weeks later.

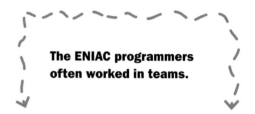

The ENIAC programmers often worked in teams.

ENIAC PROGRAMMERS PROJECT

Attorney Kathy Kleiman first learned about the ENIAC programmers when she was a student at Harvard University. She wrote papers on female "computers" of the mid-twentieth century. When ENIAC's 50th anniversary was announced, Kathy learned that the original ENIAC programmers weren't invited to the celebration. She created the ENIAC Programmers Project to tell their stories. Kathy recorded oral histories and pushed for recognition for their accomplishments. She continues to speak about diversity in computer programming. Listen to Kathy Kleiman speak about women in computer programming history in her TEDx Talk.

Connect . . . .

🔍 Kathy Kleiman TED

At first, the women weren't even allowed to see ENIAC. They didn't have security clearance. Instead, they were given wiring diagrams, blueprints, and charts! That's how they were supposed to figure out how to program ENIAC.

Finally, they were allowed to work with the machine in the 1,500-square-foot room where ENIAC lived. The 30-ton monster was 9 feet high and covered three sides of the room. It included 6,000 switches, 1,500 relays, and 18,000 vacuum tubes. And it could calculate more than 1,000 times faster than a human.

Programming ENIAC

Soon, the six women knew the machine better than the engineers. The programmers realized that the key to programming ENIAC and keeping it running was to break big problems into small steps.

The 18,000 vacuum tubes that made ENIAC so fast were always burning out. A burnt-out bulb meant that ENIAC couldn't do its job. Jean and Betty developed a system to locate and replace a burnt-out vacuum tube within 15 minutes.

There were 18,000 vacuum tubes like these on the ENIAC.

credit: Erik Pitti (CC BY 2.0)

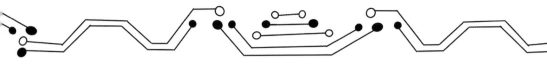

World War II ended before ENIAC could offer much help, but the Army decided to introduce ENIAC to the world. Of course, ENIAC began acting up the day before its first public demonstration. The women worked most of the night to get it working. There were many, many late nights dedicated to keeping ENIAC in working order.

Two demonstrations were held on February 14, 1946. The first one was for journalists. The second was for important scientists and military officers. The programmers weren't introduced, nor were they invited to celebrate ENIAC's success at the dinner that evening. The women were invisible.

> **"** Yet the tale of ENIAC's programming by a group of young women has all but been erased from computer history. **"**
>
> —**The Computers**
> documentary movie

Although the war was over, there was still work for ENIAC to do, and some of that work was top secret. In later years, the women would suspect they had something to do with development of the hydrogen bomb, a very powerful nuclear weapon.

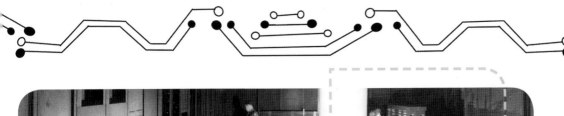

ENIAC introduced the modern age of computing. For five years, it was the only electronic computer operating in the United States. And it served the Army for nine years.

The ENIAC. Can you imagine having to use this machine instead of a laptop?

For the 50th anniversary of ENIAC, University of Pennsylvania undergraduates recreated the computer. What was once a room-size computer could now be contained on a computer chip in the palm of your hand.

After ENIAC

ENIAC was moved to Aberdeen, Maryland, in the late 1940s. Ruth and Frances went with it. Frances became head of the computer research branch, while Ruth went on to teach programming to others.

> **❝** The ENIAC programmers inspired me to stay in computing at a time when there were few women in my programming classes and every signal was telling me that computing was not a field for women. **❞**
>
> —**Kathy Kleiman**, founder of ENIAC Programmers Project

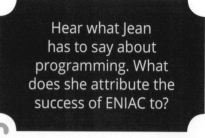

Hear what Jean has to say about programming. What does she attribute the success of ENIAC to?

Connect . . . .

🔍 Jean Bartik video

Jean, Betty, and Kay continued to work with the men who had built ENIAC, turning their focus to a new computer called the Binary Automatic Computer, or BINAC. Later, Grace Hopper worked for the same company that built BINAC.

Their next project was the Universal Automatic Computer (UNIVAC)—the first commercial computer. The U.S. Census Bureau became the first customer to use it, but the UNIVAC became known worldwide when it correctly predicted that Dwight D. Eisenhower would defeat Adlai Stevenson in the 1952 U.S. presidential election.

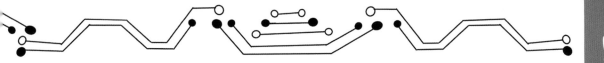

The women all had long careers with computers and received many awards for their work. Despite the lack of early recognition, all six programmers were inducted into the Women in Technology International Hall of Fame in 1997.

As the only ENIAC programmer born outside the United States, Kay received recognition from her birth country as well. The Irish Times referred to *her as the "Irish mother" of computer programming.*

BLACK GIRLS CODE

Electrical engineer Kimberly Bryant launched the organization BlackGirlsCode in 2011. BlackGirlsCode was created to show the world that African American girls can code—and do a whole lot more. Workshops, after-school programs, and camps introduce coding to young girls living in communities lacking computer science classes. The organization is committed to bridging the "digital divide." Within two years, BlackGirlsCode was working within seven states in the United States in addition to Johannesburg, South Africa. And they are expanding. BlackGirlsCode plans on teaching coding to 1 million girls by 2040.

Listen to one student talk about what BlackGirlsCode has done for her at this website.

Connect . . . .

🔎 Colgate Black Girls Code

Meet Alice

WHAT BETTER WAY TO LEARN PROGRAMMING THAN THROUGH TELLING STORIES? ALICE IS A PROGRAMMING LANGUAGE USED TO TEACH PROGRAMMING TO KIDS FROM MIDDLE SCHOOLS TO UNIVERSITIES. ALICE IS ABOUT TELLING STORIES. IT ALSO INCORPORATES VIRTUAL REALITY IN PROGRAMMING EXPERIENCES.

1 Alice is free from Carnegie Mellon University, but it does need to be downloaded. Get permission from an adult to download.

You can find three different versions available for download here.

🔍 get Alice

2 The Alice Project site is full of tutorials, lessons, and projects. Explore a little or continue on for quick instructions on how to create animations in Alice.

YOUR FIELD KIT CHECKLIST

✓ **COMPUTER WITH INTERNET ACCESS**
✓ **PAPER**
✓ **PENCIL**

3 Create a storyboard. A storyboard is visual representation of your story. No computer needed here. Just sketch it with a pencil and paper. Think of it as a way to plan and organize what you want to do.

4 Build your scene. Go to the Alice gallery. Here you will find locations, characters, and props you can use.

5 Create a programming script from your storyboard. This will help you plan what code you need to make it happen.

6 Ready, set, animate! Use the code editor to build your animation. Start with the basic dialogue. Then, add character moves and gestures.

7 Preview your animation. What do you think?

Try This!

If you're like most programmers, you'll want to do some tweaking. But don't forget to share your creation with others.

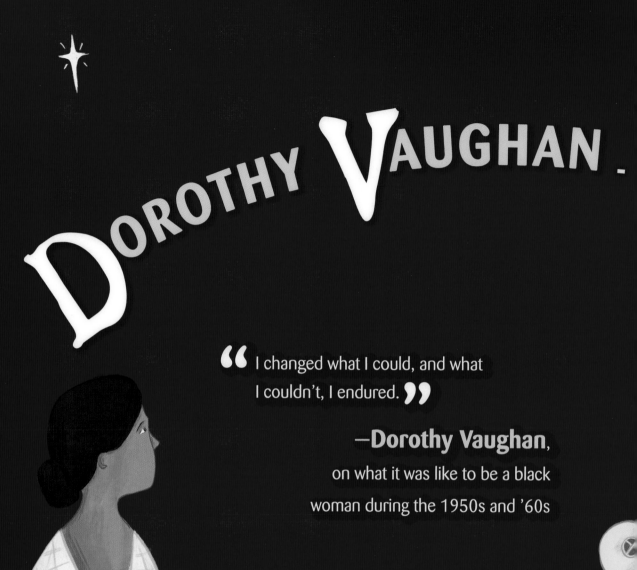

DOROTHY VAUGHAN

"I changed what I could, and what I couldn't, I endured. "

—**Dorothy Vaughan**,
on what it was like to be a black
woman during the 1950s and '60s

63

Date of Birth:	Place of Birth:	Date of Death:	Famous for:
September 20, 1910	Kansas City, Missouri	November 10, 2008, age 98	Expert programmer in the early days of NASA. One of the first African American supervisors at Langley

Early NASA Programmer

THINGS WERE CHANGING.

Dorothy Vaughan could see it coming. The National Advisory Committee for Aeronautics (NACA), where she had worked for 15 years, was becoming the National Aeronautics and Space Administration (NASA). Rumors were that segregation might end as well, and white and black people would be allowed to work together.

Dorothy Vaughan

credit: NASA

Dorothy was distracted by the sight of one of the largest machines she had ever seen indoors. It was a computer, one that could take her job away. But Dorothy didn't dwell on that. She saw an opportunity to learn something new. Few people seemed to know how to program and operate the machine. Why not her?

See what Morehead Planetarium and Science Center has to say about Dorothy Vaughan.

Connect . . . .

Morehead Dorothy Vaughan

TIMELINE	1910	1943	1949	1954	1958
	Dorothy Johnson is born on September 20.	Dorothy begins working at NACA, which is a segregated company.	Dorothy is appointed supervisor at West Computing.	The U.S. Supreme Court declares school segregation unconstitutional in its ruling on *Brown v. Board of Education* of Topeka, Kansas.	NACA becomes NASA.

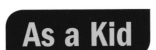

As a Kid

Dorothy Johnson was born on September 20, 1910, in Kansas City, Missouri, and when she was seven, her family moved to Morgantown, West Virginia.

School was easy for Dorothy. She graduated from high school by age 15 and went straight to college. She attended Wilberforce University in Ohio, the first American college to be owned and operated by African Americans.

SEPARATE BUT . . . EQUAL?

In 1896, the U.S. Supreme Court ruled that it was legal to have separate but equal schools for different races. However, people knew the segregated schools really weren't equal. They weren't as well funded as schools for white people. In 1954, segregation was outlawed in schools. It would take another 15 to 20 years for all schools finally to be integrated.

By the time Dorothy turned 20 years old, she had two degrees—one in mathematics and the other in French.

1964	1971	1983	1992	2008
The Civil Rights Act is passed, making discrimination based on race illegal.	Dorothy retires from NASA.	Guion "Guy" Bluford is the first African American astronaut to fly in space.	Dr. Mae Jemison becomes the first African American female in space.	Dorothy passes away on November 10.

New Jobs

After college, Dorothy worked as a high school math teacher for African American students. She married Howard Vaughan in 1932. They had six children. Called Dot by her friends, she stayed busy as a mother, homemaker, and math teacher until 1943.

That was when Dorothy saw an advertisement for African American mathematicians. World War II had started and mathematicians were needed. President Franklin D. Roosevelt signed an order that prohibited discrimination in the defense industry. Dorothy filled out an application in the spring of 1943.

Use Google's Made with Code to create a message for equality.

And then, see what girls are doing with code at Google's Made with Code.

Connect . . . .

🔎 Made with Code Equality

🔎 Made with Code mentors

While she was waiting, the school summer break started. Dorothy didn't earn enough from teaching to take the summer off. She began working at Camp Pickett's laundry boiler plant, washing soldiers' laundry. It would get so hot and humid in the plant that going outside into the 100-degree heat of central Virginia was an improvement.

Months later, Dorothy had started back to school when she received her letter from NACA. They wanted to hire her as a human computer. She quit her teaching job. She couldn't turn down a job offer for more than double the money she had been earning!

This job would let her save money for her children's education.

> **"** Possessed of an inner confidence that attributed no shortcoming to her race or to her gender, Dorothy welcomed the chance to prove herself in an academic arena. **"**

—**Margot Lee Shetterly**,
in her book, *Hidden Figures*

Dorothy was among the first group of African American scientists and mathematicians hired by NACA. She thought her new job as a mathematician at the Langley Memorial Aeronautical Laboratory was temporary. Mostly likely, she would return to being a high school math teacher when the war ended.

NACA's first wind tunnel, 1921

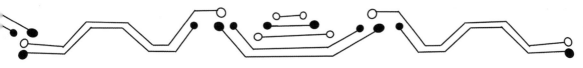

Langley was more than 100 miles from where she lived. Since the job was temporary, she saw no reason to move the family. For $5 a week, she got a room closer to work and two meals a day. When she could, she visited her family or brought her children to stay with her for a few days. When Dorothy was still working at Langley a year later, she moved her family to join her.

While the law said that African Americans would be hired, there was nothing said about working conditions. Dorothy was assigned to West Area Computing—only African American women worked on that unit. The East Area Computers were made up of white women only.

The West Area Computers had separate work and dining areas and separate bathrooms.

NASA was an early employer of female African American computer programmers, including Melba Roy Mouton.

credit: NASA

Dorothy worked with other African American women doing calculations for the engineers' experiments. The teams of engineers worked with models of aircraft flown in gigantic wind tunnels that tested their durability.

In 1949, Dorothy became NACA's first African American supervisor to the West Area Computer group. The two previous supervisors had been white women. Her role meant she assigned the women to different projects. She also continued working on special projects. With other computer supervisors, she developed a handbook for calculating machines.

Dorothy did more than calculating and supervising. She also advocated for the female computers, no matter what their race. If someone deserved a promotion or a pay raise, she spoke up.

Change is Coming

In 1947, NACA bought an electronic calculator from Bell Telephone Laboratories. The electronic calculator used paper-punched tape as inputs. It generated answers 16 times faster than humans. It also shook the entire building when it was operating!

Hidden Figures
author Margot Lee
Shetterly writes that "being on
the leading edge of integration was
not for the faint of heart." How did
Dorothy Vaughan demonstrate this?

Wonder
hy?

Although most calculations were still done by hand, Dorothy realized that her electronic co-worker could someday take her job. She also knew that integration was right around the corner—African Americans and white people were going to be working together and competing for the same jobs. The people with the best skills would win.

Dorothy began taking computer classes after work and on weekends. She encouraged other West Area Computers to do the same.

Dorothy Vaughan is on the far left of this gathering of human computers.

Whenever she had an opportunity, Dorothy visited the IBM 704 in the chilly room in the basement. The temperature was set low to keep the vacuum tubes from overheating.

NACA to NASA

Congress passed the Space Act of 1958, leading the way for NACA to become NASA. A memo was sent out on May 5, 1958. The West Area Computing unit was no more. Segregated facilities were to be a thing of the past.

Dorothy joined the new Analysis and Computation Division (ACD). This group was made up of men and women of various races who all worked on computers. Not only could the computers do calculations, they also did simulations.

Dorothy learned a new programming language, Formula Translator, better known as FORTRAN.

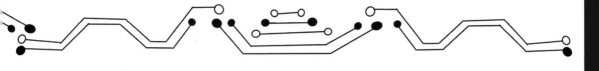

FORTRAN was the first programming language to open up programming to people other than mathematicians. The 10-person team at IBM that developed FORTRAN included one woman, Lois Haibt (1934–).

Dorothy reinvented her career and became an expert FORTRAN programmer. Because of her programming skills, she worked on important projects, such as a program that developed reliable launch rockets that made it possible to launch satellites and manned space flights.

NASA still uses a version of FORTRAN. And people still use the older versions of FORTRAN for older projects such as *Voyager 1* and *2*. Two Voyager spacecraft launched in 1977 are still sending us data about the solar system and beyond.

Dorothy Vaughan's Impact

Dorothy retired from NASA in 1971. Her contributions to computer programming and NASA remained a little-known fact until Margot Lee Shetterly published *Hidden Figures* in 2017. *Hidden Figures* is the story about African American women in the early days of NACA and NASA. The book was also made into a movie.

Dorothy spent her retirement years being active in her church and music programs and volunteering. She passed away on November 10, 2008, at 98 years old. She didn't live to see the recognition for her role in computer programming and integrating the space industry.

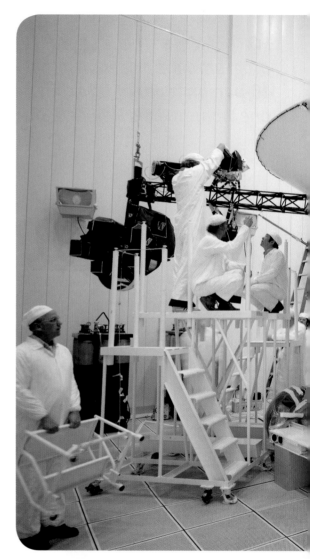

NASA's *Voyager 2* Testing

credit: NASA/JPL

While Dorothy's programming skills were critical to the American space program, she also demonstrated that African American women could be successful both in the space industry and in computer programming.

What do NASA employees have to say about the influence of the women featured in *Hidden Figures*? Check it out at this website.

Connect . . . . .

Try This! HTML

LOOK AT MOST WEBSITES, AND WHAT YOU SEE IS USUALLY THE PRODUCT OF THREE DIFFERENT PROGRAMS: HTML, JAVASCRIPT, AND CSS. BOTH JAVASCRIPT AND CSS OPERATE WITHIN HTML.

HTML stands for HyperText Markup Language. This programming language uses ordinary text to describe a page. It's fairly simply to use. HTML uses hidden keywords called tags. These keywords are between < >. Tags have an opening < > and an ending </ >. In between the tags are content. You might also add values and attributes.

!DOCTYPE tells a browser you're using the HTML5 version. At its most basic, a web page has the following tags.

```
<!DOCTYPE html>
<head>
<title>Page Title</title>
</head>
<body>page content goes here</body>
</html>
```

Do you see the patterns? Try it yourself!

YOUR FIELD KIT CHECKLIST

✓ **COMPUTER WITH A BROWSER
AND INTERNET ACCESS**

1 Create a new document in a text editor. Computers come with built-in text editors. On PCs, this is a program called Windows Notepad. On a Mac, it's Text Edit. There are also other text editors.

You might want to create a folder for your HTML projects.

2 Copy the tags from above into a file. These are your starting tags for any project.

Write about a subject that interests you. Maybe it's your favorite book, game, or place to visit.

3 Replace "Page Title" with the title of what you're writing about. And then, right after <body>, start writing your content.

Project continued to next page ⟶

4 Now look at what you just wrote. How about a few headings? A heading is shown by <h1> large heading title </h1>. You can create headings of different sizes, defined by numbers. An h1 is the largest size heading, h6 is the smallest.

5 Do you have paragraphs? Of course you do! Use <p> at the start of every paragraph. End each paragraph with </p>. If you want a line break, use just <br>. There is no beginning or end to a line break.

6 Want to make a list? Create one using bullet points with:

```
<ul>
    <li>Item 1 </li>
    <li>Item 2 </li>
</ul>
```

If you prefer a numbered list use <ol> for ordered list instead of <ul>.

7 Add an image. We all like to look at pictures.
Use <img src="source of file here" alt=add a description explaining the image">

8 Where can the reader find more information? Provide a link using <a href="url">name you want to assign to url</a>.

9 Save the page. You might want to name it "first html project." The automatic file extension in a text editor is .txt.

10 Then SAVE AS and save your file with the .html extension. You could name it webpage.html. Close your files.

Find the html file and click on it to open. It should open in your default browser. If you get an error message, then there are errors in your code. Go back and look at it.

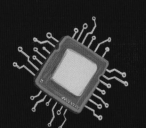

Try This!

- **Common mistakes are not using both opening and closing tags.**

- **You must remember the forward slash in the closing tag, too.**

- **Don't forget to use quotation marks around image file names and website addresses.**

- **The quotation marks show the browser the source of the content.**

- **Every programmer does a lot of troubleshooting.**

MARGARET HAMILTON - - - -

> **"** When I first got into it [computer programming], nobody knew what it was that we were doing. It was like the Wild West. There was no course in it. They didn't teach it. **"**
>
> —**Margaret Hamilton**

ON JULY 20, 1969, 600 MILLION PEOPLE GATHERED AROUND THEIR TELEVISIONS ALL ACROSS THE WORLD TO WITNESS A HISTORIC OCCASION.

They watched astronaut Neil Armstrong become the first human to walk on the moon.

What few people knew was that one of the greatest achievements of the twentieth century almost didn't happen!

Just minutes before the lunar module *Eagle* was set to land on the moon's surface, an alarm went off. At such a critical point, mission control might have stopped the mission. However, thanks to computer programming done by computer scientist Margaret Hamilton, Neil Armstrong was still able to take those historic steps.

With help from Margaret Hamilton, the *Eagle* landed on the moon.

credit: NASA

Margaret Hamilton with some of her code for the Apollo missions.

credit: NASA

TIMELINE	1936	1958
	Margaret Heafield was born on August 17.	The National Aeronautics and Space Agency (NASA) is formed.

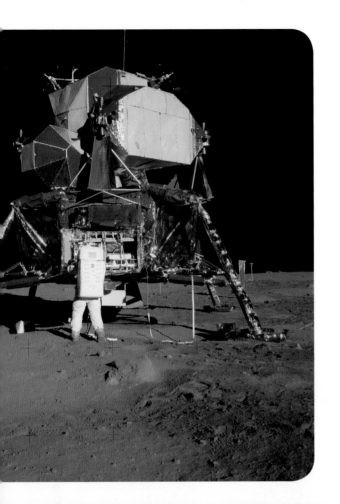

66 Our astronauts didn't have much time, but thankfully they had Margaret Hamilton. Margaret led the team that created the on-board flight software that allowed the *Eagle* to land safely. **99**

—President Barack Obama

1959	1961	1963	1969	1976	1983
Margaret begins working with code at computer labs at MIT.	President John Kennedy announces that the United States will have a man on the moon before the end of the decade.	The MIT Instrumentation Lab gets a contract with NASA. Margaret is hired to program onboard computers.	On July 20, the *Apollo 11* mission lands a spacecraft on the moon. Astronauts walk on the moon.	Margaret leaves MIT and NASA for private industry. She cofounds Higher Order Software.	Sally Ride is the first American woman in space.

As a Kid

Margaret Heafield was born on August 17, 1936, in Paoli, Indiana. She describes her father as a philosopher and a poet who talked to her a lot about the universe. Margaret realized that math was useful when thinking about the universe. She enjoyed poetry and philosophy, but when it came to solving problems, she looked to math, including algebra, geometry, and calculus.

And Margaret liked solving problems. She wondered about many things, such as why boys and girls weren't treated the same. And why weren't there more female baseball players and scientists? She did her part by playing baseball while growing up. And she continued studying math.

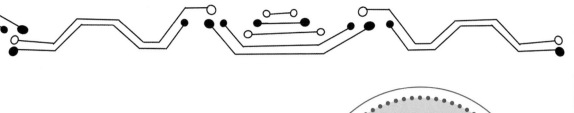

How important is diversity in school and in the workplace?

Wonder **hy**?

It seemed only natural that she would study math in college. She was often the only girl in her math and physics classes. Her goal was to become a math professor.

A female math professor at Earlham, Florence Long, was a role model to Margaret.

The First Software Engineer

While at college, Margaret met and married her husband and became Margaret Hamilton. After school, she became a high school math teacher. She and her husband decided to take turns working and going to school for advanced degrees. While her husband went to law school, Margaret began working at MIT's new Lincoln Laboratory in 1959.

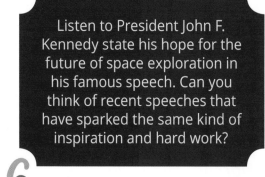

Listen to President John F. Kennedy state his hope for the future of space exploration in his famous speech. Can you think of recent speeches that have sparked the same kind of inspiration and hard work?

Connect . . . .

🔎 Kennedy space speech

Margaret quickly realized that computers could help with answers to questions about the universe. She began writing code, the instructions for computers. At first, these programs were for predicting weather.

Margaret moved to another MIT lab, the Instrumentation Laboratory. This lab provided aeronautical technology to NASA. The code for the projects she worked on grew more complicated! Margaret wrote the software for the program that identified enemy aircraft.

Margaret was often the only woman in the computer lab, but she was so involved with her work that she rarely noticed.

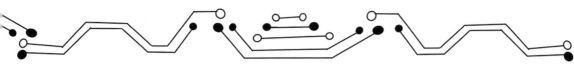

She became an expert in systems programming. There was no job title to accurately describe what she was doing, so she invented one—software engineer.

To the Moon

During the 1950s, the United States and the Soviet Union were in a race. It was a space race, and the Soviet Union was winning.

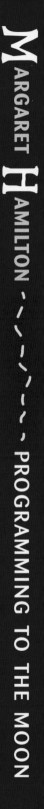

A replica of *Sputnik I*, the Russian satellite that sparked the "Space Race."

President John F. Kennedy gave a speech to Congress on May 25, 1961. He said it was time to land a man on the moon, and that the United States would do that by the end of the decade.

66 We choose to go to the moon . . . and do the other things, not because they are easy, but because they are hard; because that goal will serve to organize and measure the best of our energies and skills, because that challenge is one that we are willing to accept, one we are unwilling to postpone, and one we intend to win, and the others, too. **99**

—President John F. Kennedy, 1961

This announcement was in Margaret's mind as she considered going back to school. She was set to attend nearby Brandeis University for advanced math degrees, but then she heard that MIT was going to work with NASA to develop software to send humans to the moon. That was a project she had to be a part of!

Margaret was interviewed and hired on the same day. Work started in 1963.

Hear Margaret talk about how she ended up as the first programmer on the *Apollo* project.

Connect . . . . . .

𝒫 Makers Hamilton video

Two portable computers had to be invented for the spacecraft. One for the command module, and another for the lunar module, named the *Eagle*. And Margaret was responsible for the onboard flight software.

In addition to her challenging work, Margaret was now a mother. There were many evenings and weekends when her young daughter came to work with her. The work was very consuming! One night, Margaret left a party and hurried back to the lab when she realized a piece of code needed fixing.

By 1968, there were approximately 400 people working on the *Apollo* software. Everything they did underwent lots of testing. Programmed punch cards would be processed overnight on a giant mainframe computer that simulated the *Apollo* landing. Margaret's team analyzed and fixed any mistakes that came up.

On October 14, 1966, the *Saturn V* rocket heads for Launch Pad 39A in preparation for a trip to the moon.

credit: NASA

Once the astronauts were in space, there could be no mistakes. Margaret had to think of everything that could possibly go wrong—such as human error, loss of power, and going off course—and then have a fix ready.

In fact, her daughter helped with this. When playing astronaut, her daughter selected the pre-launch program while the simulator was in "flight." The program crashed. Margaret created a fix.

Buzz Aldrin on the moon

credit: NASA

Gutsy Girls Go for Science: Programmers

Mission control after the successful moon landing

credit: NASA

While millions of people watched the *Apollo 11* mission on their televisions, Margaret watched from mission control. Minutes before the landing on the moon, error messages began going off. Then, the 1202 alarm went off. This meant the computer was being overwhelmed with too many tasks.

A switch had been flipped to change the computer's priority system to a radar system. The software overrode that command based on Margaret's programming. The guidance computer needed to shed less important tasks and focus resources on the highest-priority task—steering and landing the lunar module. The program worked, allowing Neil Armstrong and Buzz Aldrin to safely land on the moon.

The software was also adapted for use on the space shuttle and the first fly-by-wire systems in aircraft. Fly-by-wire technology led to computerized navigation systems that are now found on all commercial and military aircraft.

Margaret became head of the software engineering division at the Instrumentation Laboratory until it became an independent laboratory.

" One should not be afraid to say, 'I don't know' or 'I don't understand,' or to ask dumb questions since no question is a dumb question . . . to stand alone or to be different; and not to be afraid to be wrong or to make and admit mistakes, for only those who dare to fail greatly can ever achieve greatly. **"**

—Margaret Hamilton

What does Margaret's quote about daring to fail mean to you? Can you think of times when you have dared to fail? Can you think of moments when you didn't take a chance out of fear?

Wonder **W**hy **?**

Private Industry

Margaret left MIT in the mid-1970s to develop her own business. She co-founded Higher Order Software in 1976. She was CEO for eight years. In 1986, she started Hamilton Technologies Inc. Both of these businesses focus on programming and software.

TECHNOLOCHICAS

Latinas are a very underrepresented group in computer science and programming in the United States. In 2016, only 2 percent of Latinas worked in the computing field. Developed by the National Center for Women & Information Technology (NCWIT), TECHNOLOchicas raises awareness about technology careers for Latina girls and their families. An important part of the program is introducing Latinas currently working in computer technology or studying computer science in school. This revolving group of computer science mentors tells their stories in person and online. You can learn from them at this website.

Connect . . . .

🔎 TECHNOLOchicas

Margaret believes that software engineering helps people be more creative and better problem-solvers. It also taught her the importance of learning from mistakes and turning them into positive results.

On November 22, 2016, President Barack Obama awarded Margaret Hamilton the Presidential Medal of Freedom for her programming contributions to *Apollo 11*. The Presidential Medal of Freedom is the highest award a civilian can receive.

Try This! HTML

DO YOU HAVE A SMARTPHONE OR TABLET? IF SO, YOU HAVE SOME EXPERIENCE WITH APPS! MOBILE APP USE IS AT AN ALL-TIME HIGH. PEOPLE OF ALL AGES, INCLUDING KIDS, HAVE GREAT IDEAS FOR APPS. APPS CAN ENTERTAIN, EDUCATE, AND SIMPLIFY OUR LIVES.

How about you? Do you have a good idea for an app? Then, let's get started with this Hour of Code project, Making Apps with Javascript.

Get an adult's permission to use the technology in this project.

1 Think of an idea. If you already have an idea, skip to number 2. If not, do some brainstorming. Do you use some apps that could be improved?

YOUR FIELD KIT CHECKLIST

✓ **MOBILE DEVICE (iPHONE, ANDROID, iPAD)**

✓ **HOUR OF CODE WEBSITE**

🔎 hour code app

2 Look into an app store. Perhaps there are two different apps that might work as one app? The idea isn't to copy someone else's work, but to look at what works and what doesn't work and what could work better.

3 Think about what would make your life simpler or more enjoyable. Perhaps there's an app for that?

4 Go to https://hourofcode.com/codehsjsapp. Watch the video for an introduction.

Download the Expo app from an app store, the QR code in the tutorial, or at the Hour of Code website. The Expo app offers developer tools for creating in JavaScript and React Native. One of the main benefits of Expo is that it works with both Android and iOS devices.

Project continued to next page ⟶

5 Continue with the Hour of Code tutorial or explore the Expo site for examples, sample projects, and tools. Don't know where you want to start? Stay with the tutorial or go to "Get started with Expo" for step-by-step instructions.

6 Create a free account.

7 Press "Project." Choose "New Project." Select "Tab Navigation." Give your project a name, then click "Create." A basic template and tools are being downloaded. When it's ready, you'll see "React packager ready" in the XDE logs.

8 Take the XDE Tour. It can be very helpful.

9 Find the developer menu and get creating. The Expo site has FAQs, how-to documents, and other resources for help.

10 Preview your app by opening "Expo Client" on your device. Use it to scan the QR code printed by "Export Start". You may have to wait a minute while your project bundles and loads for the first time.

How did you do? Is your app performing how you want it to? What can you do to improve it?

JADE RAYMOND

In the programming world, Jade Raymond is a rock star. People are so excited to meet her that they line up to ask for her autograph. That's because Jade has developed popular video and online games such as *SIMS* and *Assassin's Creed*.

Jade loved playing video games such as *Donkey Kong* as a teen. Her enjoyment continued as an adult. After earning a computer science degree, she went to work as a programmer at Sony and later EA. It was at EA that she began working as a video game producer. In March 2019, she was named a vice president at Google, in charge of a new video game streaming service.

Jade won the Legend award at the 2019 New York Videogame Awards. In her acceptance speech, she talked about how happy she was about "a light being shone on the great women in the industry."

ADAPT: to make something useful for another purpose.

ADVOCATE: to speak out for.

AERONAUTICS: the science of designing and building aircraft.

ALGEBRA: a type of math that uses letters and other symbols.

ALGORITHM: a series of steps to complete a task. There can be different algorithms to do the same thing.

ANALYSIS: a careful study.

ANALYST: someone who interprets data.

APP: a program that runs on a phone, tablet, or other computerized device.

ASTROLABE: an early instrument used to make astronomical measures.

BALLISTICS: the study of the movement of projectiles.

BINAC: Binary Automatic Computer; an early electronic computer.

BINARY CODE: a base-2 number system (digits 0 and 1), used by computers to store data.

BIT: the basic unit of information storage in a computer, consisting of a zero or a one.

BLUEPRINT: a model or detailed plan to follow.

BRAINSTORM: to come up with many ideas quickly, without judgment.

CALCULATION: a mathematical determination of the number or size of something.

CALCULUS: a branch of mathematics that deals with calculating things such as the slopes of curves.

CENSUS: an official count or survey of a population that records various details about individuals.

CHEMISTRY: the science of how substances interact, combine, and change.

CIRCUIT: a path for electric current to flow, beginning and ending at the same point.

COBOL: Common Business Oriented Language; a high-level programming language used for business applications.

CODE: another name for a computer program or the act of writing a computer program.

COLLABORATION: working with others.

COMMAND MODULE: for *Apollo*, the spacecraft that carried astronauts to the moon and back.

COMMISSION: in the military, a written order giving rank.

COMPILER: a computer program that translates language into a language a computer can understand.

COMPUTER: a device for storing and working with information. Before digital computers, people who worked with numbers were often called human computers.

COMPUTER BUG: a mistake in code that causes unexpected problems.

COUNTERCLOCKWISE: in the opposite direction to the way the hands of a clock move.

DEBUGGING: figuring out all of the problems with a computer code so the system will run successfully.

DEVICE: a piece of equipment, such as a phone, made for a specific purpose.

DIGITAL: the use of the binary number system for text, images, or sound; allows data to be used on a computer.

DISCRIMINATION: the unfair treatment of a person or a group of people because of their identity.

DIVERSITY: when many different people or things exist within a group or place.

DURABILITY: being able to last for a long time.

ENGINEER: someone who uses science, math, and creativity to design and build things.

ENIAC: Electronic Numerical Integrator and Computer; the world's first general purpose computer.

ENLIST: to join or get someone to join, often one of the armed forces.

EXPERIENTIAL: learning from direct observation or activity.

FACTORY: a place where goods are made.

FLY-BY-WIRE: a semi-automatic computer system for controlling the flight of an aircraft or spacecraft.

FORTRAN: Formula Translation; a high-level computer programming language often used for scientific computations.

FREQUENCY: the number of radio waves that pass a specific point each second.

GENDER: male or female, and their roles or behavior as defined by society.

GEOGRAPHY: the study of the earth and its features, especially the shape of the land and the effect of human activity.

GEOMETRY: a branch of mathematics that deals with points, lines, and shapes and where they are in space.

GPS: stands for Global Positioning System, a network of satellites that can be used to find your location on Earth.

HUMIDITY: the moisture in the air.

HYDROGEN BOMB: an extremely powerful bomb that's force comes from energy released when hydrogen atoms combine to form helium atoms.

INTEGRATE: to bring people of different races together.

JACQUARD LOOM: an automated weaving loom invented in 1801 that used punch cards.

LOGIC: the principle, based on math, that things should work together in an orderly way.

LUNAR MODULE: for *Apollo*, the spacecraft that landed two astronauts on the lunar surface and returned them to the command module.

MACHINE CODE: programming language consisting of binary instructions that a computer can respond to directly.

MAINFRAME: a large and powerful computer.

MANUAL: a book of instructions.

MANUALLY: by hand.

MATHEMATICS: the study of ideas related to numbers. Mathematicians study mathematics.

MEASLES: an infectious disease that results in a fever and a rash.

METAPHYSICIAN: an expert in the branch of philosophy that deals with the fundamental nature of reality.

MISSION CONTROL: a command center on Earth that helps astronauts on their mission.

NASA: National Aeronautics and Space Administration, the U.S. organization in charge of space exploration.

PARALLELOGRAM: a four-sided shape with opposite parallel sides.

PATENT: a government license that gives an inventor or creator sole right to make and sell a product or invention.

PHILOSOPHER: a person who studies truth, wisdom, knowledge, and the nature of reality.

PHYSICS: the science of how matter and energy work together. A physicist studies physics.

PRIORITY: something that is more important than other things.

PROGRAMMER: a person who writes computer programs. Also called a coder.

PROGRAMMING LANGUAGE: a language invented to communicate instructions to a computer.

PROMOTE: to raise someone to a higher position or rank.

PROSPEROUS: financially successful, wealthy.

PROTOTYPE: a working model or mock-up that allows engineers to test their solution.

PUNCH CARD: a card with holes punched in it that gives directions to a machine or computer.

RACE: a group of people that shares distinct physical qualities, such as skin color.

REBELLIOUS: fighting against authority or those in charge.

RECRUIT: to get a person to join; also someone who recently joined the armed forces or another group.

RELAY: a device that makes changes in an electrical circuit in response to other changes.

RESOURCES: something you can go to for help or support; can also be something useful or valuable to a place or person.

SATELLITE: a spacecraft sent into orbit; can also be a moon that travels in an orbit around a larger heavenly body.

SCHOLAR: a person who is highly educated in a subject.

SCRIPT: in computer programming, a script is a program or sequence of instructions that is interpreted or carried out by another program.

SECURITY CLEARANCE: special permission given only to people who are approved to know or see secret things.

SEGREGATION: the practice of keeping people of different races, genders, or religions separate from each other.

SHORT CIRCUIT: a situation in which a current takes the path of least resistance. It may result in an electric shock.

SIMULATION: a copy or imitation of something before the real act.

SOFTWARE ENGINEER: a person who develops software in a systematic method.

SOURCE CODE: a text listing of commands to be compiled or assembled into an executable computer program.

SPACE RACE: the competition between the United States and the Soviet Union to achieve the greatest accomplishments in space exploration.

STANDARDIZE: to make everything the same.

STORYBOARD: a visual representation of a story that can include drawings, directions, and dialogue.

SWITCH: in computers, a device that turns on or interrupts the flow of electricity in a circuit.

TECHNOLOGY: the tools, methods, and systems used to solve a problem or do work.

TENURE: guaranteed permanent employment, usually for college-level professors.

TRAJECTORY: the path of an object moving under a force.

TRIGONOMETRY: a branch of mathematics that studies the properties of triangles and their functions.

TUTOR: a person who gives private lessons to a student.

TUTORIAL: a routine that allows a person to instruct oneself in using software.

UNIVAC: Universal Automatic Computer; the first commercial computer produced in the United States.

VACUUM TUBE: an electronic component that looks like a lightbulb. It was used as an on/ off switch in early computers and other appliances.

VALET: a personal attendant who looks after a man's clothes; can also be an employee in high-end hotels.

VIRTUAL REALITY: an interactive environment that looks three-dimensional through a computerized device.

WAVES: Women Accepted for Volunteer Emergency Service, the American female volunteers with the U.S. Navy.

WIND TUNNEL: a tunnel built so airplanes can be safely tested in high winds.

BOOKS

Bodden, Valerie. *Programming Pioneer Ada Lovelace (STEM Trailblazer Bios)*. Lerner Publications, 2016.

Coding Projects in Python. New York: DK Publishing, 2017.

Gonzales, Andrea, and Sophie Houser. *Girl Code: Gaming, Going Viral, and Getting It Done*. Harper Collins, 2017.

Hutt, Sarah. *Code It! Create It!: Ideas & Inspiration for Coding (Girls Who Code)*. Penguin Workshop, 2017.

Robbins, Dean. *Margaret and the Moon*. Alfred A. Knopf, 2017.

Saujani, Reshma. *Girls Who Code*. Viking/Penguin Young Readers, 2017.

WEBSITES

Alice: alice.org
Black Girls Code: blackgirlscode.com
Girls Who Code: girlswhocode.com

Google's Made with Code: madewithcode.com
Hour of Code Activities: code.org/learn

QR CODE GLOSSARY

Page 18: hourofcode.com/googlelogo

Page 26: sydneypadua.com/2dgoggles/lovelace-the-origin-2

Page 42: youtube.com/watch?v=JEpsKnWZrJ8

Page 51: bletchleypark.org.uk

Page 54: youtube.com/watch?v=Zevt2blQyVs

Page 59: computerhistory.org/revolution/birth-of-the-computer/4/78/2258

Page 60: youtu.be/qVuTZhr_szY

Page 61: alice.org/get-alice

Page 65: youtu.be/KfHHu9lhMPI

Page 67: madewithcode.com/projects/change/equality/code

Page 67: madewithcode.com/mentors

Page 76: nasa.gov/modernfigures/videos

Page 87: vimeo.com/225868529

Page 89: makers.com/profiles/596e0f42bea17725160a95c1

Page 96: technolochicas.org/filtro

Page 98: codehs.com/editor/hoc/video/558818/3846/2654?